Vitality Training for Older Adults

A POSITIVE APPROACH TO GROWING OLDER

Bruno Geba

A RANDOM HOUSE • BOOKWORKS BOOK

Copyright © 1974 by Bruno Geba
All rights reserved under International and Pan American
    Copyright Conventions.

First printing, November 1974 in cloth.

Typeset by Vera Allen Composition Service, Hayward, California
    (with special thanks to Karin and Irene)
Printed and bound under the supervision of Dean Ragland, Random House

The publisher wishes to acknowledge the special advice and extra energy
    offered by Eugene Rush, Helen Ansley, Gay Luce, for their reading
    of the manuscript.

This book is co-published by Random House Inc.
                             201 East 50th Street
                             New York, N.Y. 10022

                         and The Bookworks
                             2043 Francisco Street
                             Berkeley, California 94709

Distributed in the United States by Random House and simultaneously
published in Canada by Random House of Canada Limited, Toronto.
All orders should be sent to Random House.

Library of Congress Cataloging in Publication Data:

Gebá, Bruno Hans, 1927-
    Vitality training for older adults.

    "A Random House/Bookworks book."
    1. Middle age—Psychological aspects.   2. Aged—Psychology.
3. Mental hygiene. I. Title.
DNLM: 1. Breathing exercises—Popular works.   2. Geriatrics—
Popular works.   3. Hygiene—In old age—Popular works.
WT104 G293v 1974
BF724.6.G4   158'.1   74-8055 ·
ISBN 0-394-49453-9

Manufactured in the United States of America

To

Maria, Anona, and Mark

ACKNOWLEDGMENTS

I would like to express my sincere appreciation to my long time associate Eugenia Gerrard. Without her untiring initiative as the Director of the Project for Older Adults this book could have never been written. I also want to thank my wife Suzanne and my friend Don for their essential support and encouragement.

CONTENTS

PREFACE

"I am a mimic." When I looked at my parents' middle years and saw them good, I expected mine to be good. Now I am middle aged and my life *is* good. But I look at my parents' old age and . . . .

Like father, like son. The cultural web is held together by the thread of imitation. We live our lives copying those persons close to us. As children we imitate openly. This is obvious. But we never stop imitating. Most of our mimicking we do without being aware of it, by social osmosis you could say. Long before we get a glimpse of who we are, we are that person already. And long before we can prepare to be old, we are old already. Old age can be ignored and protested only so long. And then we are caught, like spiders in our own web.

We need a new mythology of aging. The days when old age was synonymous with wisdom are long gone. Gone also are the days when elders were treated with dignity and respect because they *were* wise. They were, after all, our only connection with our past. Before the advent of books, newspapers, radio, television, films, tapes and records people relied on the memories of their elders. The old remained needed and wanted until their very last days. It was worthwhile to be old. It was honorable. But advanced technology and mass media have taken over the function of recording and preserving the past. Experts in different areas of specialization have taken the place of the sage. The wise old man has been replaced by the educated, flexible youth. Like son, like father.

But if the son precedes the father, then the natural order of life is reversed and there is no visible end. Therefore, if dying is purposely hidden and denied, it is equal only to defeat. Aging then is the process of being defeated and should be avoided at all costs. In this framework, symptoms of aging are treated as if they were symptoms of disease—either medicated or, perhaps worse, ignored. It is this reversed imitative attitude—the old mimicking the young—that turns the process of growing old into a nightmare.

We need to change our attitude about growing old. Through an invigorating attitudinal change, new values can be created. They can lay the foundation for a new mythology of aging. The initiative for this change must come from older adults. There is no time to look outside ourselves for help. The solution must come from within us. By allowing yourself to experience yourself growing old, you will discover your own solutions and will act accordingly.

And that is what Vitality Training is all about: a method which assists in changing a person's defeatist attitude into a vital one. It is a gentle way—a way of going with life, of going with growing old and all that is associated with it. The solution to your living in every phase of life is within your-self. You are your solution.

Once you change your attitude and learn to help your-self, you can teach other older adults how to help themselves. The approach is positive all the way. You, with your vital at-titude and the way you live, can serve as a model for everyone around you. You can return the order to its rightful sequence by revitalizing the aging process and making it acceptable once again. Your children will look to you for the way to live a vital old age. Like grandfather, like son.

I want to share with you an experience I had a couple of months ago. One of my trips as a consultant brought me to New Orleans. I was walking around in the French Quarter and ended up on Andrew Jackson Square. This is where a brightly-colored painting from an outdoor gallery across the Square suddenly caught my eye. I walked over and was look-ing at it when an old man came up behind me. He was a short, stocky guy with a straw hat. He asked if I liked the painting. "Yes," I replied, "I like it very much. I noticed it from across the street. It has something very exciting and vital about it." "I'm glad you like it," he said, "You know I only started to paint three years ago." "Really?" I exclaimed. "May I ask how old you are?" "I'm eighty- eight," he said without hesitation. "I started to paint when I was eighty-five. You might say I changed my profession at eighty-five.

My wife is the real artist in the family. When I made my first attempts on canvas, she told me in no uncertain terms that they were not art. But I hung my pictures on the wall anyway. And to my surprise, they sold, or perhaps I shouldn't say surprise— somehow I always knew I would paint and that people would like my pictures. My pictures make people happy. Now they are buying them, and on top of everything else, I enjoy painting. Plus, I meet people from all over the world who come here to vacation.''

I noticed that he signed the pictures ''Judd,'' so I said to him, ''Judd, would you wrap this picture for mailing?'' He suggested that we go across the street to a frame shop to have it wrapped. So we walked over and after we waited about fifteen minutes, the owner finally said, ''I'm sorry I can't wrap the picture for you; I'm just too busy. I don't have time today to do this type of work.'' I turned to Judd for another solution saying, ''I can't take the picture with me since I have a number of other stops before I return home.'' ''Well,'' he looked thoughtful, ''Don't worry. I'll wrap it and mail it. Just give me your address. I'll insure it and get it off to you. '' Then he looked up from under the rim of his straw hat and said, ''I'm not going to give up on this sale, you know. I'm not a loser. I'm a winner.''

He certainly was! And there are many other older adults who have changed as much and who are winners. They changed because they found out that they could improve the quality of their own life by themselves in many ways. After visiting different specialists and trying all kinds of methods they rediscovered their own power. Some of them came to our office for support. We helped them to change their attitude through a system which we call vitality training. In the following chapters I will tell you about the practice and the process of this exciting method.

THE EVERYDAY PRACTICE

Introduction

You can resist your own aging process or you can go with it. You can have either a defeatist attitude or a vital attitude toward it. But our society is basically anti-old. It is an "agist" society. It has a defeatist attitude about growing old. Of course, we are all the products of this type of attitude. "Young is beautiful." "Young is where the action is." "Think young." On the other hand we express our negative attitude toward aging in phrases like "old cogger, old fool, old geezer, little old ladies, old bags, old nags, old hags, a sweet old lady, or an old bitch." If you are an older man and accompany or marry a younger woman, you are "a dirty old man" or a "cradle snatcher." Furthermore, sex in our society is not for older adults. You are supposed to have outgrown sex a long time ago! If you listen long enough to this kind of attitude, you start believing it and before you know it you are living it. You are too old for sex, too old for your job, and just too old to be around.

When a person loses his youth, he loses his looks, his

agility, his speed, his job, his spouse, his hair or whatever else seems important to him. And when you lose something, you usually look outside yourself to regain or replace it. This is the solution society has taught us to pursue when we want to change a situation. If you have a job you don't like, you look for another. (But now you are old and you cannot find a new job.) If you have a bad marriage, you can get out of the marriage and find a new partner. (But now you are old and no one else will want you.) So if you look around outside yourself for solutions to aging, you become desperate because you can't find any solutions. You lose your center and thereby lose your vital attitude. You become imbalanced. You develop a defeatist attitude. But if you can't rely any longer on changing your situation, you can always change your attitude. This is true about your job, your marriage, your age, your looks, your sex life, your illness, or whatever.

The true test of vitality training is the ability to transfer a change in attitude from a structured learning process into everyday living. The following chapters will introduce you to methods which have helped people to cope with problems that seem to recur again and again in their lives as older adults.

Beauty is in the Eye of the Beholder

A couple of months ago, a former student of mine paid me a surprise visit. Two years had gone by since we had last seen each other. At that time, she had worked with me for several weeks following the sudden death of her husband. When she first visited me, she was having a hard time adjusting to being single again after being married for 45 years.

My secretary announced the name of the surprise visitor, but it didn't sound familiar to me. Then she stepped into my office and I recognized her immediately. "Betty! Nice to see you! I've thought of you many times and wondered what you've been doing." She gave me a big hug and then moved away, looking me over from head to toe and exclaiming, "Hey, it's good to see you. The same old Bruno!"

We sat down and began to talk about old times and what had happened since we last met. She told me that she had remarried three months before and was very happy. "Remember," she mused, "how preoccupied I used to be

with my appearance? Walter's death really threw me for a
loop. I felt so alone and old. Boy, did I ever feel old! I kept
telling myself that I shouldn't have any wrinkles; I shouldn't
have gray hair; I should dress younger and look younger. As
long as I had Walter I felt secure. But when he died, a feeling
of having to be somebody else overpowered me. This must
happen to lots of older women?''

    ''Not only to women,'' I said, ''but to men too. I used
to work with a man who was extremely concerned with his
baldness. His lack of hair was not only a question of looks but
it began to threaten his manhood. First he dyed his hair, then
he tried a transplant, and finally ended up with a hairpiece.
But he was continually nervous about it. You know what he
ended up doing? He turned his weakness into his strength. He
shaved his head completely, got a nice tan and grew a beautiful white mustache! Not only does he look very distinguished but he says he feels better than he has in the past
twenty years.''

    Betty nodded, ''I remember only too well the terrible
feeling when I realized that I was trying to look an age I
couldn't possibly be. I worked so hard to be beautiful and
young looking that I almost lost myself. Can you believe at
my age that I joined the Golden Owls, an older women's
consciousness-raising group? That did the trick. What I'm
saying is a part of being myself is not only being female but
being old. It has its own beauty!''

    ''And you're a living example,'' I told her.
''Remember the old adage,'' she replied, '' 'Beauty is in the

eye of the beholder'? Well, I started believing it!''

The classical approach to any form of disease is to fight conflict with conflict, resistance with resistance. If you have a migraine, you take a pill against it. If you have hemmorhoids, you use a cream against them or you undergo an operation. If you are mentally ill, you are treated against your neurosis. The orientation, in other words, is exclusively against disease, against illness. What we forget is that the migraine, the hemmorhoids, the neurosis are all symptoms of inner conflicts. Anything that is done against these symptoms also goes against the conflict that is at the bottom of them. So one ends up fighting conflict with conflict.

The orientation of vitality training is *toward health* instead of *against illness*. We feel it is better to yield than to resist. When we yield, we surrender to our nature. We surrender to all the forces that work within us to promote our health. Basically, this is the difference between treatment and prevention, between therapy and prophylaxis. We call this principle the paradoxical nature of change. We change by first becoming who we are rather than who we want to be.

In the natural process of growing old, we have to allow ourselves to be as old as we are. Otherwise we only make ourselves sick by trying to maintain the type of young appearance we have long outgrown. Then we become the victims of our own conflict.

"It Doesn't Pay to be a Martyr"

Susan's eighty-four year old husband has suffered from cancer for the past three years and still manages to hold onto life. She has had to make a lot of adaptations to his being ill. She used to sleep in the same room with him until about six months ago. "Before that," she said, "I practically had to give up my own life. So I decided to move upstairs and let Marty live by himself downstairs in our apartment complex." She said that when she first did this, all her friends put her down. How could she leave her husband downstairs all by himself? But she insisted. "Being so close to him all the time," she maintained, "used to get me down. I couldn't move at all. I couldn't invite anyone over. Everything had to rotate around him, but he couldn't participate in anything I did. So I was just wasting away next to him. This didn't do him any good either." So she decided to assert herself and follow her true feelings. The funny thing was, her new-found zest for life spilled over on her husband. As she put it, "He told me after a week had gone by that he liked the new arrangement because it gave him some independence too. Apparently he didn't like having me around him all day either.''

Almost without exception, whenever a person goes against his real feelings, he makes them known anyway by very subtle means. No matter what he says or does or how well he tries to cover them up, his feelings come through. And other people are adept at picking up those hidden feelings. We are not totally hypnotized by words or social games and are often able to receive two conflicting messages at the same time. For instance, the words we hear may say one thing: ''Marie, I just love that new hat of yours!'' But the slight facial grimace says something else: ''But, Marie, it just isn't your style!'' A situation like this puts you in a double bind. It is confusing—it is hard to know which message to believe. Whenever we are in a double bind, we can't win either way. It is a very disturbing experience. Furthermore, even if we can figure out which message carries the genuine feelings—as in the frivolous example above—we have trouble acting accordingly.

A couple of months ago I had a session with a woman I had been working with. Two years after her husband's retirement he was diagnosed as having cancer. After living in this situation with him for a year and a half, the woman felt she needed outside help.

After a few general words with me, she came right out and said with a trembling voice, ''I am very upset. My husband has started to bleed again. You know, it is his intestinal cancer. I have so many negative feelings, I am embarrassed to share them with anyone. Of course, I am also scared and worried what will happen when my husband dies.'' ''Have you ever talked with him about his condition?'' I asked. ''Yes,'' she answered, ''but in rather general terms.''

I then asked her if she had ever shared any of her deep feelings with him—her resentment and fear. Her immediate response was, ''No, I can't do this. He is in such bad shape already. I can't burden him with my fears too.'' I asked her if she didn't think he knew what her feelings were after having lived with her all those years. She hesitated and then said rather quietly and with conviction, ''Yes, perhaps so. He caught me crying once and I'm sure he put two and two together. I also know that he has lots of the same feelings. A good talk might do a lot for both of us. But how can I get started?'' Well,'' I said, ''Why don't you just start with the things that are easiest for you to say and then play it by ear?'' We left it at that.

When she entered my office three days later, I could tell immediately that she was feeling more relaxed. Even before she sat down she started to talk. ''I feel so much better. So does my husband. We had a long talk and after I began to tell him some of my worries it was he who carried the conversation. You were right. He knew all along that I was scared, and he was also aware of the resentment I carried around. In all the years we have lived together we never talked like this. We also cried together and held each other for a long time. I feel like somebody took a big weight off *my* chest. And I know *he* is more at peace.''

I have met many couples where one of the partners has given up expressing his wants in the marriage. He has become a martyr by deciding that it is not worth the hassle, or that it is unfair to his spouse to say what he really thinks or feels. But his true attitude shows up in the form of subtle resentments.

I have concluded from years of experience that going against one's own feelings rarely benefits anybody. Even under circumstances that seem to justify protecting another person, it really doesn't pay to be a martyr. The truth seldom hurts; but even if it does, *it is better to have an ending with pain than pain without end.*

"Long-Lived and Still Winning"

I first met Mr. Slingsby during a training workshop on alcoholism. He has since been coming to me on a regular basis for three months. Before his retirement he was a salesman for a large paint company. Now, in his early seventies he lives alone, his wife having been killed in an automobile accident some three years previously. Since her death he has had a hard time accepting his retirement. "I just can't get the thought out of my mind," he said. "It seems just yesterday that I would get dressed and drive to my job. I was wanted, needed, and paid well besides. Then retirement came, my wife died . . . and overnight I'm a bum!"

His "forced exile," as he called it, left him lonely and depressed. Otherwise he was in good health and had no serious physical complaints. "I feel so low all the time," he complained, "that I don't even have the energy to mow the lawn. I have lists of things I have to do, and quite a few things I really want to do—like go to the ball game or play poker with the guys. Instead, I hang around the house, making myself miserable. When I start wishing my wife were still with me, that's when I begin to feel sorry for myself and turn to the bottle. I can't seem to break out of this dilemma.'' Then his eyes would stare into space, looking nowhere, and his face would get an empty, forlorn look. Such depression and lack of energy are perhaps the most common complaints we hear when talking with older adults. They are the most prominent symptoms of the anti-old attitude that permeates our society.

After I had worked with Mr. Slingsby for about two months in my office he began to shed some of his defeatist attitudes. One day he talked about taking up golf again, so we arranged to have our sessions on the golf course. Surprisingly enough, it seemed easier for him to talk out there than in the office. At first he only played a couple of holes with me, but the last time he felt strong enough to play a complete round! When we were finished he remarked, ''If you had told me half a year ago that I would be playing golf again, I would have said you were crazy. But here I am and I feel great. The more I do, the more energy I have and the more time I have for other things. I even discovered the Triple L Club.'' ''What's that?'' I inquired. ''Long-lived Libbers,'' he laughed. ''It's a group of older men and women that get together to help each other—like getting legal advice and solving all kinds of problems. We call ourselves ''long-lived'' instead of ''old'' and are determined to overcome the negative, self-defeating attitude toward growing old that is around.'' ''That's great. And you are right!'' I said. ''When you are *old,* you are deteriorating; but when you are *long-lived* you are experienced. When you are *old,* you are losing; but when you are *long-lived,* you have already won!''

The Myth of Insomnia

We don't really know how to sleep. We just sleep. Or more correctly, we are being slept. Sleeping, like all of our other bodily functions, has certain natural patterns. As we grow up, however, we are often influenced by social patterns, and no longer do things simply because our body tells us to. We eat because it is time to eat, because our mother or our hostess calls us to eat or because it is just convenient to eat. We even eat because there is nothing better to do! We ignore the voice of nature and become victims of obesity, indigestion, heart trouble, and so forth.

A similar situation exists in the sleeping process. We don't go to bed because our body tells us to. We go to bed because it is 11:00, because our television program ends or because our mother, wife, or roommate goes to bed. Even worse, we go to bed because there is nothing else to do! We think we *should* sleep. We create a conflict within ourselves when we can't sleep and we call it *insomnia*.

My associate works regularly with a group of older

adults. The other day the problem of insomnia was brought up for discussion. When the question "How do you sleep?" was asked, people answered almost unanimously: "Terrible!" "What do you mean by 'terrible'?" she said. One woman really expressed the sentiment of the group when she answered, "I wake up two or three hours after I've gone to bed. Then I lie awake for a long time—sometimes for hours. It is a miserable experience and I feel very lonely lying awake by myself. I ponder many depressing thoughts; I can't wait for the morning to come. I'm perfectly content during the day but my nights are turning into a horror show." "Are you doing anything about it?" my colleague asked. "I've tried several kinds of tranquilizers and sleeping pills, but I feel that I shouldn't have to take anything. After all, I'm a healthy woman and I hate to take drugs to begin with." Then the group was asked if they felt tired during the day. "Not at all," most of them replied. "When do you go to bed at night? When do you get up?" my associate inquired. "I go to bed around 10:30 and get up at 7:00," one man answered. "This has been my pattern for years. I never used to have any trouble sleeping." "Well," commented my colleague, "this might just be the very reason why you are having this problem." "What do you mean?" he asked, looking at her curiously. "I mean simply that you may be trying to sleep too much. What you think of as sleeping well was how you slept when you were younger. Then you may have slept through the entire night without waking up."

Life in our modern culture is set around this day and

night cycle. Except in the larger cities, there are few provisions for nighttime activities outside the home. "But I do live
in a city," one woman said, "and I wouldn't dare venture out
alone at night." "I see," my colleague remarked, "so basically what you have to do at night is read, watch television or
go to bed?" "Exactly" she replied, "and there isn't much of
value on the TV at night anyway—at least nothing that would
appeal to the older set like me." "Yes, I know," my
associate answered, "our values and models are not geared
toward people who live longer and more vital lives. As we
noticed in other areas of our society our ideals are strictly
youth-oriented." "I understand what you mean," the woman said. "I am still operating on a youth model, so to speak. I
try to force myself to fall asleep, which only compounds my
problem. Instead of telling myself it is time to go to bed, I
should ask myself, 'Am I really sleepy?' Is that it?" "That's
it," my associate replied. "You listen to your body. If the
message you get is 'I'm not sleepy,' then don't go to bed.
Otherwise you create a conflict by overruling your body.
You make yourself an insomniac by thinking that you should
be asleep when you are not sleepy at all."

   "I have a similar problem, it seems," said one
gentleman. "It is not difficult for me to fall asleep, but I wake
up after a few hours and can't go back to sleep." "I see,"
said my colleague. "You are tired enough to fall asleep
initially but, by waking up, your body tells you, 'I've had
enough sleep; let's do something else!'" "Maybe so," this
man replied, "but another voice keeps telling me 'It's only

three o'clock. Go back to sleep.' Besides what could I do if I got up? It is hard enough to fill the day with meaningful activities without trying to think up something in the middle of the night when the rest of the world is fast asleep.''

When we reach a certain age, society removes us from the mainstream of life. As a consequence we have more time on our hands than ever before, a problem which is further compounded by the fact that we now need less sleep than when we were younger. What is the answer? If you will listen closely, the body will tell you to use this extra time for other things—things like music, creative writing, painting, prayer, silent meditation, handcrafts or just listening to the wind. There is plenty to do when you grow older. The problem is that we have adopted the attitude in our culture which says older people have no energy and there is nothing to do.

Being old is relatively new in our society. Never before have there been so many older adults. Today they comprise over 10% of our entire population. And with the lowering of the birth rate and the increase in life expectancy, this figure will climb even higher. We are in desperate need of new values and lifestyle patterns. As in the specific case of sleeping, older adults are going to have to find their own lifestyle model and set their own pace.

Participate in Your Pain

"The pain is killing me," Joe told me, stroking his chest and abdomen with both hands. "I am hurting all over. I've seen three doctors about it but they blame it on my age and a minor arthritic condition. One doctor told me that I worry too much, and gave me some pills to take. They didn't make the pain go away. I got those funny side effects which kind of worried me. Anyway, I don't like swallowing drugs, so I stopped taking them."

I nodded my head and responded, "Do you realize that when you talk about pain, you treat it as if it were something outside of you—a stranger to your body that doesn't belong to you?" He looked surprised. "The truth is, your body creates the pain," I added. "You own it. And if you own a thing, you are free to do whatever you want to with it. This is true about your voice, your age or your pain. You do have a choice, you know."

"Could you give me an example?" Joe replied. "Sure," I said. "Although you may not be able to eliminate pain completely, I know one thing—you can change the quality of your pain by changing your attitude about it. Take a friend of mine who received his medical training in Boston. He is an obstetrician. He told me that during his internship he assisted many Latin women giving birth. In their culture, it is accepted, even expected, that women shriek and cry out during childbirth. These women heard from their mother, grandmother, aunts and sisters that the pain is so excrutiating that a woman will cry out in agony and beg for mercy when she labors. So they are indeed in great pain and they cry out endlessly in labor and in birth. Then my friend moved to an upper-middle class New England community where a 'lady' does not embarrass herself or those around her with emotional outbursts, but maintains her composure at all costs. There he observed women giving birth by clenching their fists and biting their lips. But none of them would utter a loud noise. Then he came to California and began assisting with natural childbirth where the women were all prepared in advance to go *with* the birth process. This natural approach often made the new mothers insist that the sensations they felt were not pain. They experienced only how it felt to give birth. Their *attitude* made all the difference!''

''Now I understand you,'' Joe said. He sat quietly for a moment and then continued, ''When you talked about childbirth I had to think about the birth of our children. Do you know they kept my wife in the hospital for 10 days each time! She was even kept flat on her back at home for several days afterwards, even though she had relatively easy births with all three of our children. But like you say, the attitude was different then. You went to the hospital to give birth the same way you went to the hospital with a serious illness.''

"Exactly,'' I responded. ''I never thought of it this way. But you are right. Instead of teaching women how to go *with* childbirth, the philosophy was one in which doctors and mothers actually went *against* it. Women were anesthetized and kept from participating actively in a natural process. They handed all of their power over to the doctor, the anesthesia and the drugs.''

"What you can do with a natural process like childbirth, you can also do with pain, with disease, with aging, with anything. A change of attitude can make a lot of difference,'' I continued. "What you're telling me is that I *could* do something about my pain,'' Joe said. "Yes, exactly,'' I replied. "When you get older, your body shows its wear and tear in many different ways. Some organs get worn out, the joints don't move as well anymore, the eyesight weakens, you have aches and pains. All these are 'natural' processes. Still, nobody thinks of them this way. Instead, they are treated strictly as diseases, like childbearing, as you pointed out before. So you end up fighting your *disease* with drugs and gadgets, without actively participating in the aging process. Don't misunderstand me! I am not saying you shouldn't use all the help modern medicine has to offer. All I am saying is that you should try to make *positive* use of your own power.

Toward Health and Sexuality

Disease has a purpose. In my private practice, over and over again I see people using their *dis-ease* to express feelings they can't admit in any other way. With a sore throat they keep themselves from talking. Through bad breath they say "Don't come close to me."

Vitality training gets you in touch with your disease. By allowing yourself to fully experience your feelings and actions you discover the attitude you are expressing through them. You realize that you no longer need to protect your true feelings. You change your attitude about yourself. I know many people who use sleep as a means of escape. They try to escape the emotional pain of dealing with something. Even when they are awake, they are half awake. They vegetate and try to forget whole parts of their lives. This avoidance is a sure road to depression and senility.

Rufus used to be an accountant for a department store and has been retired for almost ten years. "When I was still working," he told me in our first session, "I used to have a hard time turning my head off. Without sleeping pills, I couldn't have made it. But now, since my wife died, I have just the opposite problem. I can't keep myself from sleeping. It is as if I want to sleep my life away. I take naps and still sleep through the night. But I am tired all the time and very depressed. Sometimes I just want to say goodbye to the world.''

Since that first confession, Rufus has been working with us nearly four months. He has made lots of changes in his life. During our last session he said, ''You know, Bruno, when I started working with you I was really skeptical. All that 'attitude' business. I thought it might be for the birds. Well, you sure have made a believer out of me. Remember when I first came here? I was so depressed, I thought I was a hopeless case. I'm sure glad I stuck it out. I guess the breathing helped me more than anything else. It got me in touch with my feelings. Apparently when my wife died I turned them off. Now I have discovered my sexuality again and with it a need for closeness and intimacy. When I first felt these sexual feelings again I told myself, 'Cool it. This is for the young. Don't make a fool out of yourself, you old rooster.' But I met Julia. She came at just the right time in my life. Or was it me that found her at the right time? Whichever, I made life work for me again. And you know what is so funny?'' he laughed. ''After all that sleeping I did, now I am so awake that I sometimes have a hard time falling asleep. Crazy, isn't it? Quite a switch after all that depression!''

Rufus' story is a perfect example of the complex interrelationship between a person's attitude and his problems of living. But the idea that one can influence his own life by changing his attitude sounds strange to many people. And yet, within a sick life there is always a healthy life that continues to resist disease. Healing takes place when we allow ourselves to get in touch with the natural movement toward health. In this way we heal ourselves, or even better, we keep ourselves from getting sick.

Passing thru the Gate

The other day, during our first interview, Mr. Stone began relating a story to me about his late wife. It was an extremely painful experience for him to talk about her. He didn't want to judge their marriage, but while she lived they had never been able to verbalize their feelings. He told me, "Our life together was always a struggle, starting on nothing, raising a family during hard times, high-risk jobs with odd hours and little pay, then finally, finally we arrived. It seemed that for the first time since we met, we had enough time and money to sit back and enjoy ourselves. Then it happened. We learned that my wife had cancer and was dying. I couldn't believe it." As he went on, tears rolled down his cheeks and he struggled to find the right words. After a while he continued, "I have been thinking a lot about those last weeks with my wife. I wish we could do it all over. We had such a hard time talking about our situation. Now I know we both were ready to share our feelings and be together. But somehow we never got to it. I felt I had to protect her from knowing how upset I was and how it scared me to be left without her. We didn't face the issue. Now I am left with all the things I wanted to tell her.''

Stories like this are more common than most people think. They may concern husband and wife, as in the Stone's case, but more often they concern relationships between children and parents or single older adults and their friends. So much remains unsaid; important feelings never get a chance to be expressed. Furthermore, we are taught to approach death with a defeatist attitude. Dying in our society is not considered a natural condition of life. It is treated rather like a personal failure, something to be avoided. Death is resisted like disease and fought to the last moment. We live in a ''dyist'' society. *Death* is a dirty word. Many times we act as though it is the disease that dies and not the person. Too many older adults die in isolation with no opportunity to be close to another human being. Older adults, and dying persons in particular, are ''untouchables.'' This separation plays directly into the defeatist attitude of an individual. Movement, sexual interest and general curiosity about life diminish. The old and dying often assume a mask-like face, a huddled, self-clutching posture and other depressive withdrawal symptoms.

Nobody should have to live alone and nobody should have to die alone. When I worked in Iran I came across an old Persian saying: 'There is no greater blessing than dying in the midst of friends.' I've also heard of a hospice in London which was organized to help people find comfort in the last hours of life. This place, St. Christopher's Hospice, encourages younger persons and children to visit the home. They also teach families how to keep dying relatives in comfort at home rather than in a hospital.

I know of one convalescent hospital where the members take turns sitting with their dying friends. One lady there told me that she was sitting with a friend who was in her last hours of life. As they talked, the dying woman pushed back the covers of her bed and asked her friend to lie next to her. She wanted this intimacy as she gave up her life.

In the wards of most nursing homes and hospitals there is no provision for privacy. This tends to restrict physical contact—holding and touching—which are so important to older adults and dying persons. The need of intimacy is very great at any age.

It is often said that aging is a woman's problem because women tend to outlive men. My assistant worked in one convalescent hospital where the patients were all women. These women were allowed to get closer to each other. Good friends held hands much like girlfriends in other cultures, where open demonstration of affection is permitted between females. Some of the women took naps together and rested in groups much like young girls in our own culture do today. A change of attitude such as this is desperately needed to bring human warmth and closeness into the lives of all people. Dying with a defeatist attitude is as abrupt an end as running into a wall. By changing to a *vital* attitude, the process of dying can become a preparation for passing through a gate, and the very act of dying a meaningful act of life.

THE LEARNING PROCESS

A Philosophy of Healing

Many individuals are referred to us for vitality training by physicians and other treatment specialists. We make it clear to people from the beginning that we won't treat them or take care of their symptoms, but will try to help them find new ways to deal with problems in their life situations. In other words, we are not a medical treatment center. We leave treatment to the medical doctors. Basically we are a school whose function is to assist a person in self-education.

In our area, people in the helping professions are beginning to recognize our position as an educational venture. They see us as a link between their field or specialty and their patient's actual life situation. Physicians have long been faced with the problem of what to do with and where to send patients after medical treatment has stopped or has proved to be ineffective. Doctors are aware that such people need help and that this type of help is not available within the general medical framework. Physicians and other professionals have expressed their frustration about people returning to their office over and over again looking for a kind of help they cannot give. They question the value of medicating such people and realize that drugs which dull the senses also prevent positive action toward deeper problems. And older adults in particular shy away from anything that suggests psychiatry or psychology. They protest, "I'm not crazy."

The responsibility from the beginning is not with us as teachers but with the person who comes as a student. The teacher is only a servant. He facilitates the student's responsibility, which is really his ability to respond to himself. The orientation is always positive. Instead of treating what is *not* wanted, the teacher serves the student in the process of mobilizing what *is* wanted. For example, he does not help the student combat his fatigue. Instead, he helps him activate his energy. The emphasis is on health rather than against disease. And this is the major difference between vitality training and other "therapies." (The word, "therapy," by the way, has its origin in the Greek word "therapeuein," which means "to serve." Ironically, the meaning of "serving" has almost completely disappeared in today's therapeutic settings. Today, therapy means treatment, and interestingly enough, the word "treatment" comes from the Latin "tractare," which means to pull. The idea of pulling somebody can also be expressed as manipulating somebody. And manipulation is exactly what therapy in most cases has become. No wonder older adults avoid it.)

As previously indicated, the teacher is in the service of the student. It is his job to pay attention to the student, who has within himself the answers he needs and is himself the only one who can activate them. The teacher is simply the instrument and tool of the student. And the student is always right! This situation is just the opposite of the classical doctor-patient relationship, in which the doctor is the expert who manipulates or cures while the patient remains passive and dependent.

Vitality training is based on the assumption that two tendencies of life are constantly expressed in all of us. One is the movement toward health (the vital attitude) and the other is the movement toward disease (the defeatist attitude). The teacher is the enemy of the movement toward disease. He always supports the vital attitude of the student, no matter how weak it might be. The student, however, has a choice. He can use the teacher in either direction: he can build him into his tendency toward disease or into his movement toward health. Either way, the teacher cannot do much about it. It is the student's choice. But the teacher can always support the tendency toward a vital attitude whenever it appears, for no situation is ever completely dominated by movement in one direction. In fact, I have seen many people in my life who were classified as hopeless mental cases but who got well in spite of the treatment they received. This supports the idea that the essential element of healing does not come from the outside but from within the person and is closely related to his attitude. It may seem surprising, but in some cases the patient actually uses a doctor to reinforce his own defeatist attitude to remain ill or even to become sicker. Likewise, the physician in the role of the expert can unknowingly play into the patient's defeatist attitude and support him in his illness.

Life speaks to us in many languages—through growing, feeling, breathing, sleeping, digesting, thinking, dreaming—sometimes without a voice, sometimes loud and clear; sometimes intelligently and sometimes crazily; sometimes with health and other times with disease.

Vitality training is a method of helping the student tune in to all these many ways in which life expresses itself through him. It teaches the student to harmonize with his nature and to create a more vital life for himself.

In the following chapters we will attempt to familiarize you with the process of vitality training. But first we would like to give you a general overview of our method and introduce you to our vocabulary.

The Interview is designed to create a close personal relationship between teacher and student. It is the first step of the training process which we call *Creating a Human Bond*.

Supportive Practices help the teacher to facilitate the student's inner-directed and self-appropriated re-education, through greater *Self-Awareness*. The student learns through his own experiences of touching, massaging, meditating, listening, moving, and breathing how to *Pay Attention To Himself*.

Relaxation Explorations help the student to become aware of his state of tension. He learns through his own experience how to *Release Himself*.

Movement Explorations help the student to become aware of his manner of carriage (posture and movement). He learns through his own experience how to *Center Himself*.

Energy Explorations help the student to change his state of awareness (consciousness). He learns through his own experience how to *See Himself*.

Breathing Explorations assist the student to become aware of his quality of breathing and his emotions. He learns through his own experience how to *Integrate Himself*.

Vitality Explorations help the student to become aware of his way of being (his nature). He learns through his own experience how to *Liberate Himself and Have Vitality*.

Creating a Human Bond

I work with people. A lot of information filters through me during the day. People tell me about their lives—their problems, their aspirations. They tell me about their childhood, their marriage, their joys, their disappointments and their fear of death. It is a never ending list.

George A., one of my students, tells me that he is 64 years old and a widower. He used to work for the city as a bus driver. It seems easy for him to talk to me in complete honesty about himself. I pay close attention to him, to the tone of his voice, his posture, his facial expressions, the movement of his hands, his eyes, yes, particularly his eyes, because they are truly the mirror of a person's soul. "I can't see how you can be interested in all this stuff I'm telling you," he says to me. "You must get tired of hearing the same old things over and over again." While we talk something else is taking place. Without our being aware of what is really happening, we are coming closer to each other. We have formed a bond, an area of mutual understanding, a human bond. It is created through feelings of trust, sincerity, respect and empathy. I can't really explain how it all comes about. I only know when it is there and when it isn't. The human bond is a spontaneous event. It evolves directly from person-to-person contact.

George is aware of what has happened. He tells me he has experienced an inner certainty about me. "I have a feeling that you hear me. I sense that I am also beginning to understand myself better." Yes, we hear each other all right. We have established a good relationship. Older people, more than any other age group, need such a confidant, someone to share their memories and feelings with.

They also need—and we have seen this over and over again—to be touched. Touching plays an important part in the work we are doing. The teacher uses many opportunities to establish this direct physical contact with the student. The most neutral and least threatening area to touch or to be touched is, of course, the hands. Let me illustrate this point with a story one of my assistants told me recently. This assistant is an older woman in her late seventies, extremely active in our association and a living example of what we believe in.

The following is her story:

"The other day when we visited the retirement home on Center Avenue an old lady was sitting almost completely hidden in a corner. While most of the other women in the room were chatting with each other and asking me all kinds of questions about our program, she remained extremely withdrawn. After I had talked to all the other people, I walked over to her and asked how things were going. She responded with an empty and forlorn look. Then it came to my attention that her fingernails and cuticles were in very bad condition and that a lot of rough skin on her fingers was starting to break open. So I reached for my handbag and took out my manicure set. I took her left hand and began to cut her fingernails and snip off some of the hard skin particles around her fingertips. As I did this, I asked her a few questions directly related to what I was doing like, ''Does this hurt you? Do you want me to do the other hand too?'' And this is when she said her first words, ''Yes, please.'' This is how our conversation started. She began to tell me how thankful she was to me for doing this for her. After I had finished I took some cream out of my handbag and began massaging her hands. This is when I really experienced the first emotional reaction in her. Her face became a bit flushed. She began to sit up a little bit straighter, and I recognized the strange mixture of upcoming tears and a certain delight in her eyes. She said that I really had been the first person in a long time to touch her in this way, by massaging her hands. She had forgotten how good it felt and how much she needed to be touched by another person.

Touching plays a very important role in creating a trusting and caring relationship. From our experience we can say that older people as a rule have a tremendous need to be touched because they are sorely neglected in this respect. It always amazes us after working a couple of weeks in a convalescent home to see how hugging can become a part of everyday living. Through this direct body contact the human bond is vitally strengthened and a new degree of intimacy and trust is established.

Paying Attention to Yourself

At the beginning of a session, teacher and student talk about experiences that have occurred since they last met. A typical pre-session conversation might run something like this:

Teacher: "I haven't seen you in a week. What have you been doing?" *Student*: "Well, I practiced the exercise you taught me last time and I can feel the heaviness very strongly in my lower legs. But my arms, particularly the right one, will only respond a little bit. Yesterday for the first time I felt a kind of drifting into what I think you called the energy state. It surprised me. It was a very pleasant feeling, though. But the moment I noticed it, it got away from me." *Teacher*: "That's great. Continue to practice. But remember not to force it. You will see. It will come to you naturally. Today you will learn the next routine. What else has been going on in your life?" *Student*: "Well, the rest of the week was a disaster. But strangely enough, my colitis never acted up and I haven't had a week this free of pain for a long time. I can't understand it. Somehow it didn't make sense—my life was in a turmoil, but my colitis never acted up.'' *Teacher*: ''You're saying that in spite of the bad time you had, you felt physically all right? What was it that gave you such a bad time?'' *Student*: ''Well, I had a real showdown with my wife—a kind of fight we've never had before. She irritates me a lot but I usually manage to keep the lid on. This time I blew my stack. I told her exactly how I felt and when it was all over, I must say I felt pretty good.'' *Teacher*: ''Well, from the way you tell it, you seem to have changed quite a bit as far as I'm concerned. You say that your week was terrible, but you are so outgoing talking about it. Remember, last week I had to draw every single word out of you. Your attitude sure has changed. Perhaps that had something to do with your colitis not acting up?'' *Student*: ''Yes, I have been thinking about that myself. I guess I've held my feelings in check for too many years. I really did have a bad week, but I guess it was only because I'm not used to fighting. At first I felt bad, because I thought I shouldn't talk this way to my wife. But as time went on I started to feel better and better. After the storm was over I felt closer to my wife. I was able to talk with her better than ever before. Now that I think of it,'' and that's when a big smile crept over his face, ''I know that I really had a good week. I realize now that by constantly telling myself what I *should* do, I kept myself from doing what I *wanted* to do. I kept the pain inside. Talking to my wife like I did was not easy for me. As a matter of fact, it was a pretty painful experience at the time. But I feel that my wife deserved every word I said—she had it coming to her." *Teacher*: "Yes, you *have* changed! When I saw you for the first time a few weeks ago, you could hardly look me in the eyes. You gave me the impression of a broken man. Now look at yourself. You are sitting up straight. Your eyes are sparkling and you talk with conviction. Also, what you just said about the pain is very true. By telling yourself you shouldn't say certain things you held onto something inside of yourself that needed to come out. This might have been the primary source of your colitis. Keep watching yourself and see what happens."

Student: "I will. I had to pay the price for having a fight, but keeping it all in used to hurt me even more. Now I feel that this might have been the best fight I've ever had in my life. It was a catastrophic experience for me, but something really worthwhile happened. I know it. I feel alive again!"

In our everyday living we are usually preoccupied with events that go on outside of ourselves. We react to the outside world by telling ourselves that we should do this or we should have done that. And we ask, "What will the neighbors think? How will this look to others?" Our attention is *outer* directed. We reflect the outside world in our own actions. But the moment we pay attention to *ourselves* we discover our inner processes. The student is encouraged to pay attention to sensations going on inside his body, to feelings he has or to movements he is making. The teacher assists the student in this process through verbal feedback, by having him move a certain way or by touching him.

I met Mr. Morgan during one of my convalescent

home visits. He told me he had suffered a stroke and that since then he had been forgetful and unable to remember people. During our first meeting he tended to repeat himself several times. His bright blue eyes could be sparkling one moment, and have the blank stare of a daydreamer the next. But Mr. Morgan was a very good-natured man and had a gentle way of expressing himself. We made friends rather easily. After our first interview he never got me mixed up with another person nor did he forget my name.

During our first meeting he had told me about the years when he represented a large national company in Denver. Those days for him were clearly marked by a feeling of security and prestige and I sensed that the loss of his social status bothered him considerably. He never said it directly but it was implied in nearly every word he spoke. And it was at this point that he would get an empty stare in his eyes.

I began my second session by asking him to talk about his days in Denver. He opened up more and more and even told me about some of his youthful escapades— and about silver mining and the blue blue of the Colorado skies. I had lived in Colorado myself for several years and encouraged him to tell me more about his life there. He showed me an entirely different side of himself as he recounted and relived some of his happier Colorado experiences.

Remembering that he had previously told me about trouble he was having with his legs, I said, "Remember the first time we talked, you complained that you had little feeling in your legs, that they felt stiff, and that you often worried when they got cold that you might not be able to walk again? Today I will work on your legs.'' I planned to use massage to get into closer contact with him and give him support and sustenance. I hoped that in the process he would increase his awareness of his legs. I suspected that if he would pay attention to himself and respond to his legs, he would learn that he could participate in reshaping his life, a task which he now believed beyond his power.

I asked him to sit down on the couch. I helped him take off his shoes and socks. Then I asked him to lie down on his stomach. I pushed his pantlegs up over his knees. Then I took a foam rubber pillow and put it underneath his ankles. I asked him if he was comfortable. He assured me that he felt fine. I put some massage oil on my hands and began to stroke his calf muscles. His lower legs felt stiff and hard. So I said, ''Your legs feel pretty stiff. It seems that you are still holding onto them. Put your foot into my hand.'' I took his right foot with my hand and lifted it about six inches from the pillow. Then I let go, but the leg did not drop. He held onto it. I repeated the process several times until he could let his lower leg drop into my hand.

I did the same thing with his left leg. Then he said, ''Yes, I know what you mean. I got the feeling that my knee was a hinge that was stuck. Now I can see that I really can allow myself to let my lower leg go.'' Then I massaged the toes of his foot, the arch and the sole, and I kneaded his calf as deeply as I could without hurting him or causing him to resist me. I put one leg at a time in a vertical position resting on its knee and shook out the calf muscle. After that I put my hand on his calf and asked him to close his eyes. Then I said, "Please pay attention to the area where my hand touches your calf. Are you aware of your calf?" He replied that he was and that he could feel the impression of my hand. When we tried the same exercise with his other leg he said that it was much more difficult for him to be aware of this side. I stroked his calves a few more times, readjusted his pantlegs and then let him sit up slowly.

Again I asked him to close his eyes and allow himself to pay attention to his toes, his arches, his ankles—moving his awareness up into his knees. And with that our session was finished. I helped him put on his shoes, although it was easier for him to put them on than it had been to take them off. And when he stood up he said, "You know, I can feel the soles of my feet. They feel a little warm, warmer than they've been for a long time." We then worked out a self-massage routine for him and set a date for our next visit.

Releasing Yourself

Life is tension. Without tension, there could be no life. Too little tension or too much tension interferes with the processed of life in the same way a string on a guitar interferes with the melody when it is either too loose or too tight. The right amount of tension in a human being is called relaxation. And relaxation is simply the level of tension that allows one to function normally in his environment.

The word "tension" is commonly used today to mean "hypertension" which is a state of getting too tense or too high strung to enjoy a situation or to perform well in a given circumstance. The same is true about the word "relaxation" which is ordinarily used to mean "over-relaxed" such as the state after three double martinis! A better term for describing this condition would be "collapse." *Relaxation* lies in the middle between *hypertension* and *collapse*.

Both work and play, if they are to be rewarding, must take place within this dynamic equilibrium. An athlete feels anxious and excited when he anticipates his upcoming race. If he is too tense, he cannot move with agility and if he is too relaxed he cannot perform to his capacity. The same is true in regard to drama. An actor needs a certain amount of tension to project his stage image, but on the other hand, he needs to be relaxed enough to play the part naturally.

The other day I met with Mr. Nelson. The moment he walked into my office, I could see the tension in his face. As he began to talk I noted that he always pursed his mouth between sentences. His jaw muscles were clenched and his shoulders were held up almost level with his chin. After we had talked for a while, I sensed that he was struggling to tell me something.

Finally he found the courage to bring up his problem: "I am a worrier," he said. "I worry about everything. I don't really know why I should, for we live comfortably enough. But I'm always thinking: What if this inflation keeps eating away at our income? What if our property values take a dive for the worse? What if someone in the family gets sick? . . . You just can't imagine all the things that worry me." He puckered his mouth momentarily, and then reflected, "I just feel anxious most of the time. It seems like the more anxious I become, the shorter my breath gets. Then my shortness of breath makes me even more anxious, and my anxiety makes me still shorter of breath. It's a vicious cycle! I was thoroughly examined by two doctors, but they couldn't find anything physically wrong with me. Then I finally saw your friend, Doctor Murphy, who felt that you might be able to help me to relax.''

"I always have a hard time getting to sleep, and then I am restless most of the night.'' He paused, pursed his lips and then continued, ''My wife even complains that I wake her up during the night grinding my teeth. Well, I am tired before I even get out of bed. On top of the utter fatigue, I have lately had a lot of trouble with pain in my lower back and on down into my legs.''

At this point I asked him to stand up and walk around the room a couple of times. As he walked his tenseness became even more obvious. His buttocks were tight and his legs were stiff. He held his shoulders rigid. There was no swing or sway in his body or in his walk. So I said to him, ''Close your eyes and put all your attention into your shoulders.'' Then I put my hands on both of his shoulders to make it easier for him to ''get in touch'' with them. I now said, ''Pull up on your shoulders, as hard as you can. As hard as you can and harder!'' He did it so hard that his head began to quiver. Then I said, ''Now let go of yourself. Release yourself in your shoulders, and let go. Good. Let's do the same thing a couple of times. Yes, pull up your shoulders really tight around your neck, until you feel the tightness shooting into your neck and jaw and back into your shoulders. Pay attention also to what happens in your face.''

He replied immediately, ''Yes, I feel my face all pushed together. I know what you mean.'' ''Now release yourself again,'' I said. We tried the same thing over and this time I told him to inhale as he pulled up and tightened his shoulders and exhale as he let himself go. "Keep your eyes closed," I reminded him. "And try to become aware of how it *feels* to be all tense and tight and then how it *feels* when you let go of yourself and relax. Pay attention to your breathing." After he tried it several times he opened his eyes and announced, "Yes, I feel it now. When I hold onto myself, I tend to hold onto my breath. When I let go of myself, I make a little sigh." "Right, let's try it again," I said, "but this time when you hold onto your neck and shoulders and jaw, inhale deeply. Really hold on and stay there. Okay. Now stay up there and pay attention to your buttocks and your legs." He responded without hesitation, "I feel myself pulling in." I asked him what he meant and he replied, "I'm pulling in my anus and seem to be holding onto my legs."

"Fine," I replied, "Now exhale and relax. That's enough for today. But before our next appointment, let's work out some explorations for you to do at home. They can help you *experience* your tension. Make yourself as tense as you can and then let go of yourself as much as you can. Do this with different parts of your body. Start out with your face and end up with your feet. Combine these exercises with your breathing. Take a deep breath and hold onto yourself in *tension* and then while you exhale, *release* yourself. If you should get too anxious take a deep breath, count slowly to six and exhale slowly. Do this about five or six times whenever you feel very tense. Is this clear?"

"Yes," he replied, "And I can see something else. Until now I have always tried to overcome my feelings of tension and anxiety with will-power. But my condition only got worse. It seems like I needed all my strength just to keep from weakening." "I know what you mean," I said, "This is what we have all been taught. Pull yourself together! Get hold of yourself! If you want to do something badly enough you can do it!''

This type of approach does not really work. On the bottom of all tension is our defeatist attitude. The moment we try to control our defeatist attitude with our will-power, this attitude controls us and makes us tense. Whenever we're tense and strive to control ourselves, we only increase this conflict. We fight our conflict with more conflict in the form of will-power.

"This seems to be what you have been doing with yourself, Mr. Nelson. It takes so much of your energy that you feel tired most of the time.''

Centering Yourself

Gravity is to man what water is to fish. We are constantly under its influence and yet we are rarely aware of it. Have you been conscious lately of the gravitational force acting on you? I doubt it. And yet, gravitation works *on* you and *in* you all the time. Your posture and movements are under its constant influence. The relationship between your center and the center of the earth is an indication of how you are living on this earth. You express how ''centered'' you are or what attitude you have in your posture and in your movements.

The eager person, for instance, has a tendency to lean forward, pushing his center of gravity slightly ahead, keeping himself on the move. The hesitant individual, on the other hand, is always slightly behind his center of gravity, barely keeping himself from falling on his back. I'm sure if you watch the way some of your friends walk you will get an indication of their attitude. If you feel good about yourself, your feet are planted solidly on the ground. You stand upright, ready to go, but still relaxed. You carry your chin high and are aware of what is going on inside of you and around you. We say you are "centered." Movement explorations assist you in centering yourself, in bringing your center of gravity into agreement with the gravity of the earth. When you are centered, the way you hold yourself and the way you move allow you to be *fully in this world.*

But when you are overly tense, your hips and pelvis are tight, your shoulders are pulled up and your stomach is pulled in. You lose touch with the ground and as a consequence you lose touch with yourself. All your awareness is directed toward anticipation, toward the future. You miss the present entirely! You are out of it. This is what we mean by saying that your attitude is embodied in you. How you *are* in this world shows up in your body, stance and movements, which clearly mirror your way of being. If you are preoccupied with the idea that you are too old to do anything and that your aches and pains are killing you, then you indeed *will* be too old to move and pain *will* immobilize (or kill) you.

Mrs. Egger, another of our students, is seventy-two years old. She used to work in the family delicatessen but two years ago her arthritis became overpowering. We had met with her several times and were exploring her ability to relax. Through the relaxation explorations she discovered how she had been holding onto herself. In the beginning she had told us, "I often feel that I want to do certain things, and yet I am unwilling even to make an effort to begin them." What better way was there to describe the conflict she had been having with herself?

At one of her later sessions Mrs. Egger proudly told us: "I have felt some definite improvement during the last few weeks. Almost all of my joints move easier somehow. I have been doing those relaxation explorations you showed me every day, religiously, and I must say I feel better than I have for a long time. As you know, I've been very skeptical. But now I begin to believe you."

"I think it is great that you could stick to the routine," I answered her. "Today I will get you started exploring your posture and your movements by learning to center yourself. Would you please sit down in this chair? Now close your eyes and describe to me how you experience yourself sitting in this position. Share your observations the same way you did while you were learning how to release yourself." She nodded and closed her eyes. She spoke quietly and slowly. "The one thing I am immediately aware of is that I have much more pressure on the left side of my seat and on the upper part of my left thigh than on my right side. It feels like I'm resting all my weight on the outside of my left foot. My right leg almost feels weightless. All I can feel is a strain in my right knee. But my right leg almost isn't there. My left shoulder is also tense. I seem to carry my head with my left side only. Yes, I really feel all crooked. All the strain seems to be on my left side and I'm not in touch with my right side at all. My back feels round and a little bit hunched and my chin is resting on my chest. I have the feeling that I'm breathing with the upper part of my chest, here on the left side more than the right.''

"Hold it right there," I said. "Now open your eyes. You really gave me an excellent description of yourself. I could see and feel with you almost everything you said. Close your eyes again please. Plant both of your feet on the floor, about a foot apart.'' She interrupted me, "I have a hard time bending my right knee. It hurts all the way up into my hip.'' I responded by saying, "Inhale a little bit deeper. The moment you start your exhalation, slide your right heel closer to the chair. And then try to relax yourself all over. That's right. Now your heels are close enough in. Do you feel the soles of your feet? Good. Now put your lower arms on the arm rests. Support yourself a little bit. And slide farther toward the back of the chair. That's enough. Now follow with your left foot. Tell me if you feel any changes.''

She exclaimed, "Oh, I sure do. I feel more solid. My weight is distributed more over both my thighs. And I realize now how I have been ignoring my right side lately. It really is my *pain* side. But right now I am feeling okay. I seem to be sitting up a bit straighter, too—much straighter anyway than I have been sitting in the past.'' I asked her to sit up a little bit more until she felt she was not leaning forward any longer.'' Try to swing in like a pendulum,'' I said, "so that you have a feeling you are not leaning too much forward or too much backward. Right. Start out by leaning forward again. More. More. Now pay attention to your lower arms while you straighten up.'' She was amazed. "When I was leaning forward, I began holding onto the arm rest with my hands and supported myself there. When I straightened up, it was no longer necessary to put my weight on my lower arms or hands. I feel much freer sitting this way.''

At this point, I asked her to raise her chin a little bit until she was balanced. She did so and then said, ''I understand now what you've been trying to get me to feel.'' I asked her if she was comfortable with her eyes closed and she said that she felt all right. ''Now let's do something else,'' I said. ''Close your eyes again and sit like you were sitting in the beginning of this exploration.'' ''You mean the lopsided, curled up kind of way,'' she asked. ''Right,'' I said, ''Try to get the real feeling for this position. Exaggerate your experience and *be* really lopsided and curled up. Describe to me how this position makes you feel inside.''

''I feel uneasy. I am uneasy,'' she repeated. ''It is as though I couldn't get up and do anything for myself. I'm helpless and actually in pain again. And when I am in pain I know that no one wants to be around me or help me.'' She paused and then continued, ''That's strange. The moment I said that, I felt a wave coming up in me that made me feel sorry for myself.''

I encouraged her, ''It's amazing how much insight you have into yourself. Just keep your eyes closed and stay in the same position.'' I pointed out the large mirror on the wall and asked her to open her eyes and observe herself. ''Look at yourself and the way you sit in the chair.'' ''I don't believe it,'' she exclaimed, ''Do I really look like this? I guess I look exactly like I feel.'' ''It's quite an experience, isn't it?'' I

responded. "Now please close your eyes again and assume
the other position. Get the real feeling of having contact with
the ground and with the chair. Bring your feet in just a little
bit more. Begin to center yourself the way you did before.
Picture yourself sitting like a queen." "I feel like a queen,"
she declared. "I can't believe the difference in feeling."

"Yes, I can see a touch of royalty," I joked. "Now
release yourself a little bit more in your shoulders. The feeling of a queen must have given you a feeling of power and
this powerful attitude moved into your shoulders. But a real
queen is used to power in her life—she doesn't need to hold
onto herself. So, release yourself. That's right." She brought
her neck and head into a very natural position. "Now open
your eyes and look at yourself in the mirror again." I said.
She opened her eyes and smiled, "Oh, yes. I like myself
sitting this way. You know what I'm aware of right now? My
eyes. I feel that I haven't looked out of them as straight for a
long, long time."

This was just a part of a typical session. But it will
give you the general idea of what is meant by *centering yourself,* both with *releasing* and *centering* explorations, with the
eyes closed or open in front of a mirror— standing, walking,
sitting or lying down. It is recommended for such a session
that students dress as lightly as possible, without belt or gir-
dle or other binding apparel. This will help them to both feel
and see themselves better.

Seeing Yourself

Mrs. Rogers is sixty-eight. She is a very attractive and well-groomed woman who used to be a buyer for a big chain store. When she first came for her visit, she told us: "I have been a perfectionist all my life. My biggest trouble is that I never seem to be able to live up to the demands I put on myself. Neither can anyone else measure up to the standards I set for them. I get awfully frustrated about this. My husband is now seventy-three and had a stroke two years ago. Ever since then life has been particularly difficult for me. I have become more and more irritable and resentful. My mind is a constant flux of thoughts spinning around. I can't stop thinking! Maybe this wouldn't be all so bad except that a year ago, I began having terrible migraine headaches. They used to come on about once a month, but lately I have them at four or five day intervals. I can feel them coming on. The first warning is a little nausea. Then I get a creeping feeling underneath the skin and a pulling below my eyes. I try to fight off these feelings but it doesn't really help me. In fact, I have found that trying to resist them seems to make them even worse."

Since that first interview with Mrs. Rogers, I have had three more sessions with her. We have become good friends, in fact, and have gone through a variety of the releasing and centering explorations together. At the fourth session, she said to me, "Three days ago when I felt another one of those migraines coming on, I did the releasing explorations you showed me. You know, the ones where you tighten everything around your neck and your jaw and then you release yourself. They helped me a little bit. At least it took my attention away from my thoughts. I feel if I could only stop worrying, I could lick it. All those drugs I've been taking for the past two years haven't helped me a bit. So here I am again. Last time you said we were going to do an exploration which would be more directly related to my migraines."

"Okay," I responded. "Today I'm going to explain to you the first step of a method which might make it possible for you *to help yourself* with your migraines. We call this method *energy exploration* or *how to see yourself* and we approach it initially in four steps. The first step deals with heaviness, the second with warmth, the third with pulse, and the fourth one with breathing. As soon as you can do all four of them, we will try to combine them into one whole exploration. By going through all four of these steps, you will be able to get into a special and very pleasant state of consciousness which we call *the energy state*.

You may have heard of transcendental meditation and of self-hypnosis? Both of these methods work very much in the same way as the energy explorations. They help you to relieve your tensions when your head is filled with thoughts. In order to reach the energy state you must learn to *empty your head* so to speak— which in turn will relax you and give you added energy. And I might mention that the explorations leading to this energy state cannot possibly harm you, for you will always be in full control of the situation. You are always able to slow or hasten your pace as your body dictates. You set your own rhythm!''

Then I told Mrs. Rogers, ''As we go along, as you practice at home, you will now and then drift into a state of consciousness that is somewhere between that of total wakefulness and sound sleep. Once you get into this state, you will feel relaxed and *charged with energy* . . . Later on, we will outline in detail further specific explorations that will help you get rid of your migraine headaches. For now, though, let's begin with our first routine, which concentrates on the feeling of *heaviness.''*

I asked Mrs. Rogers to take off her shoes, loosen her clothing and lie down on her back on the couch. ''If you will give me your glasses,'' I suggested, ''I'll put them right here on the table. That way you won't have to worry about them. Move a little bit more to the left. Now you are lying in the middle of the couch with your hands to your sides. Take a couple of deep breaths and with each exhalation *let go of yourself*. Inhale, exhale and let go. That's right. Now let me tell you something about this exploration. While you are doing the exploration you will have your eyes closed. I will say short sentences to you. You will repeat them sentence by sentence silently to yourself. So for instance, when I say 'My right arm is heavy,' you concentrate on your right arm and repeat to yourself 'My right arm is heavy.' Don't say it out loud. I will always leave enough time before we go on to the next sentence for you to repeat to yourself what I have just told you . . . Don't try to force yourself into getting heavy. It won't work. Just *let* yourself be heavy, in whatever part of your body you are paying attention to at the time.''

I explained to Mrs. Rogers the rest of the heaviness step of the energy exploration, answered all of her questions and went through the entire routine with her. After we had completed the routine, I let her lie quietly for a minute or so and then asked her to open her eyes. She blinked a couple of times, turned her head toward me and said: ''I don't believe it, Bruno. Do you know that I actually had a distinct feeling of heaviness in both of my lower legs. Particularly in the right one.'' ''How about your arms?'' I asked. ''No, not in the arms. It was much harder for me to concentrate on them. A lot of thoughts seemed to interfere with the sentences I was repeating. Once we were finished with them and my legs got heavy, I thought for a moment I was going to fall asleep. Just for a split second, you know.'' I assured her, ''This is the first sign of your ability to shift your awareness and reach the energy state. As we go on, it will get easier for you to recognize the moment you drift into it. Then, once you are able to get into this state of consciousness quickly and deeply you will learn to use it regularly. Is there anything else you want to share with me?''

"Yes, there is," she said. "Just before I opened my eyes I became aware of some dreamlike pictures in front of them. Trees and clouds, I think. Is this normal?" "Not only is it normal," I responded, "but once you become facile in reaching the energy state, we will encourage you to work with these images. The whole area of visualization exercises, or image explorations as we call them, play a very important role in vitality training. With their help you will not only get a more realistic picture of yourself but also of other things that seem relevant to you, like your migraine headaches for instance."

Mrs. Rogers sat up and nodded. Then she looked straight into my eyes and said, "That sounds exciting. I can't wait to get there." "You will," I responded. "All it really takes is practice. Through practice you learn to see yourself and get in touch with your spontaneous energy. By freeing that energy and making it available, you will experience relief from your headaches." As Mrs. Rogers walked to the door she turned around and said, "I am aware of some changes already. I can't quite describe what they are but my head seems lighter and my eyes feel more relaxed. This is going to work. I know it will. I'm anxious to go on further with the other steps in the energy exploration. See you on Wednesday."

Integrating Yourself

This chapter is about breathing. While energy explorations help you get in touch with your spontaneous energy, breathing explorations help you integrate this newly found energy into your body. Why breathing, you might ask? Well, most of the breathing you do throughout your life takes place without your being aware of it. Unconsciously, you are being breathed. Nature is breathing you. You can't make yourself breathe right. Breathing *is* already. But by living a certain way, you interfere with your natural form of breathing. All people do this. The attitude behind the way you live shows up in your breathing just as it shows up in your posture, your movements, your dis-ease and in all the other actions of your life.

When Mrs. Hudson came to us, she had problems with her breathing. She told us: "Since my husband died a year ago, I have had a lot of trouble with my lungs. I have been wheezing and almost gasping for air at times. What scares me more than anything are the choking sensations.

I've been treated for bronchial asthma and have been taking pills that help me control the attacks. But the pills make me so nervous. I feel as though I'd just consumed five cups of coffee. I've reached the point where I am sick of the whole thing and ready to try anything. You know, last week I left town in high spirits to have dinner with a friend I hadn't seen for almost ten years. Fifty miles out of town and halfway through an enjoyable dinner, I began wheezing. Do you know that I wheezed and coughed and cleared mucous from my throat so much that I lost my voice from laryngytis by eight o'clock. I could hardly talk to my friend, which was why I had gone in the first place. Right in the middle of a party and suddenly I'm almost an invalid! I sometimes wonder if I were stranded somewhere for any length of time without my magic pills, if I'd literally die wheezing!''

Mrs. Hudson gave us the impression of a domineering and rather impulsive woman. She told us that she used to be heavily dependent on her husband and thought she needed him to protect her and the family. But now that her husband was dead, she had become aware of some new feelings for him. In one of the following sessions she told me: ''Before his death I couldn't allow myself to have these feelings of resentment. I knew that something was eating me up but apparently I didn't want to know what it was at the time.''

After that I worked with Mrs. Hudson two more times and introduced her to the breathing explorations. After we had talked for a while, I asked her to lie down. She took her shoes off, unbuckled her belt and lay down on the couch. I put my hand on her abdomen just below the navel. Then I said, "Last week when you did the breathing explorations you inhaled and exhaled 60 times. Now instead of breaking them up into three sections of twenty cycles as we did last time, we will have two sequences of forty deep-breathing cycles each. Of course, if you feel uncomfortable any time during the exploration or don't want to continue, just interrupt. Start whenever you are ready. Inhale deeply, release yourself, and exhale, breathing only through your mouth. Inhale deeply, release yourself and exhale. That's fine. Just continue in this rhythm."

While Mrs. Hudson was doing this exploration I listened to the rhythm of her breathing, and watched the movement of her chest and abdomen. I also paid close attention to her general body position and facial expressions. By doing this I have learned to pick up a lot of information about a person on a strictly intuitive level. I usually can tell if someone doesn't feel well, long before she decides to tell me.

I continued to pay close attention to Mrs. Hudson, and after about twenty deep breaths, I asked her if she was feeling all right and if she wanted to continue. She nodded her head and I said, "Stay in touch with yourself and concentrate on your body. Wander through your body, into different areas and fish for feelings or sensations. You might find a tingling, a numbness, a coldness or a vibration." I recognized that her jaw was getting a little bit tight and that her lower lip began to quiver slightly. A wave of color also rose to her face, so I asked, "Are you aware of any special kind of feelings? Try to get in touch with those feelings. Perhaps you can recognize what they are.'' She nodded again slightly and by that time she was finished with about forty breathing cycles. I told her to slow down, to again breathe through her nose but to remain in touch with her body. After waiting for half a minute, I asked her to share the experience she had during this first part of the breathing exploration.

She opened her eyes, and swallowed a few times, ''For a moment I felt very anxious and was ready to quit,'' she said, ''but then I remembered what you told me during our last sessions when I had to stop so often, so this time I was able to allow myself to feel anxious and kept telling myself that it's all right. It worked. It really did. After that, I felt a tightening around my mouth and then a tingling around my lower lip. For one moment somewhere during this experience I thought of my husband, and I felt some sadness coming into my face. My eyes began to fill with tears and that's when you asked me to breathe regularly.''

I looked into Mrs. Hudson's face, and thought again how much more energetic and vital a person looks after this breathing routine. She had a natural flush in her face which gave her a very open appearance. I asked her if she felt well enough to continue with the second set of deep breathing cycles. She said, ''Oh, sure. I feel better now than I felt when we started. More alive, you know what I mean?'' ''Yes, I do,'' I answered, ''I can tell just by looking at you. Let's do some more, and this time let those vibrations you discovered around your mouth spread into the rest of your face. That might help you fully experience the feeling of sadness you just described. If you don't feel too uncomfortable, go with the sadness. Tell yourself, 'It's all right'—the same way you did with your anxiety in the beginning of the session. This time I am not going to talk at all during the breathing exploration so you can put as much awareness into your experience as possible. Now close your eyes and begin to breathe deeply. Inhale and exhale. From here on you are on your own.''

After about 20 deep breaths I could see that things were happening. Her mouth tightened up again, the lower lip began to vibrate slightly and a couple of tears rolled slowly down her cheeks. At that point I said softly, ''It's all right. If you feel like crying, allow yourself to cry and keep breathing.'' Then, as if on command, she began to weep, wiping the tears out of her eyes. After a short while, her deep breathing was interrupted by her crying. I didn't say a word, but let her cry quietly until she opened her eyes. She said: ''It was just like the first part of the exploration. I started to get sad, my eyes began to fill with tears and again thoughts of my husband came into my mind. This time I clearly recognized what I was sad about. I was sad that I had been so hostile toward him during our last years together. At the same time I was afraid of losing his love. I feel very guilty. I've always had a hunch that this was bothering me but I've never been able to tell anyone— not even myself. I feel relieved.'' ''I'm glad,'' I said. ''Now just close your eyes again. Lie quietly and be with yourself.''

In the case of Mrs. Hudson, it was the breathing that energized her. It increased her energy flow and thereby brought her emotions to the surface. Through breathing, she encouraged movement. She allowed herself to feel more. By having a vital attitude about her feelings, she began to get in touch with herself. She found out more about how she was in the world and what attitude she had. Through this process she brought about changes in her life.

If we don't move, we don't change! The quality of our breathing is the most basic form of emotional expression. We hold onto our breath when we are angry or in suspense. We sigh in regret or out of longing or sadness. We gasp for air when we are surprised. We whimper in fear, and express our grief in a mournful wailing. These are all ways in which the emotions that are embodied in us are expressed in the way we breathe. They are the voices of our attitude.

Liberating Yourself

Last year I gave a demonstration to members of a large adult community. During the question and answer period that followed, a very distinguished looking lady with white hair asked me, "Dr. Geba, you have talked a lot about a change of attitude but I never heard you mention anything about will power. How does will power fit into your system?" "It doesn't," I answered. "Changing one's attitude is not a simple affair. As a matter of fact, it is a rather complex process. Will power, as the word says, is using the power of your will. With it you can change activities in your life but not the attitudes behind them."

Vitality, like love, spontaneity, or personal growth cannot be forced or willed. Think back to the first four years of your life. What do you remember? A fleeting trace of the kitchen wall paper. The rays of sunlight across a porch step. Your grandmother standing in the back yard. Most people retain only fragmented, commonplace memories of their earliest years. And yet if you consider all the exciting firsts that must have happened during your earliest four years, it is amazing how little is retained. You heard, saw, tasted, moved around and had a multitude of first impressions bursting in on you. All those early experiences are much more basic than anything you are confronted with in later life. What can be more powerful than gaining independence and control over one's own body, from the movement of the bowels to the movement of the whole organism? You are being lived by your nature before you ever consciously live your life yourself. And all these early experiences are preserved within yourself in the regions referred to as the unconscious. What it is, nobody really knows. But your nature knows and you are lived by its wisdom. That's where life really is!

Al is a man in his late sixties. When he came to our clinic, he told us, "After I was retired for three years, I got very restless. I thought I should do something to earn some money on the side. And doing nothing was getting to me, so I enrolled in a real estate salesmen's course. The first couple of weeks were fun, and it was good to get out and meet people. But now I'm in a real bind. My reading assignments are really getting to me. I'm ruining practically every day plugging along, chapter by chapter, through my books. My lousy mood is affecting the people around me. Like yesterday, I had to read chapter six. There was the book lying open on my desk. I just couldn't stay seated and do it. I looked out the window. I called a friend of mine on the phone. I made myself a drink. I nibbled. That really made me mad because it blew my diet. You see, I'm trying to eat well, keep my weight down and watch the cholesterol. To make a long story short, I wasted the entire day, made myself and my wife miserable and only got two and a half pages read. This sort of thing has been going on for a week now and I'm desperate, angry, frustrated—you name it. What can I do about it?''

"You can do one of two things. You can have your cake or you can eat it. You have to choose one or the other. What makes you so uncomfortable is your indecision. Pay attention to your conflict. The one side of you wants to become a real estate salesman and the other one doesn't. It is like having one man pull on your left arm and another pull on your right. You are in the middle, in the center of your conflict, fighting both sides at the same time. But you can get yourself out of this bind. First you let go of yourself. You allow yourself to be pulled in both directions. Then you pay attention to yourself and feel which side you want to go with. Once you have decided, you put all your energies in this direction. Then the other side doesn't have a chance. You begin to move, you are no longer stuck. Which side you choose is really not important. What is important is that you resolve the conflict that immobilizes you.

"The choice is not often an easy one, I know. But release yourself and pay attention to your conflict rather than fight it. I'm sure you will find a satisfactory solution this way. Either way you decide, you will have to pay a price. You can't have one without giving up the other. But you can find out which price is easier for you to pay. Once you know the direction you want to go, go with it as much as you can.''

In Al's case I told him, "Either quit the real estate course or make the best of it. If you decide to become a real estate salesman, play the game well. If you decide that the price is too high, then quit the course and throw away your books. If you decide to continue, then an important part of playing the game well will be reading chapter six."

This is what vitality training teaches. You practice what you've learned. Through practice you develop discipline, and through discipline you gain freedom. The problem most people have in their lives is that they play the games they choose poorly, or they don't choose well the games they play. They have a defeatist attitude. And that is where their suffering comes from. The answers are not in the situations, actions or games you choose. They are always in the attitudes behind them. What makes them different is *how* you play them. Everything you want to do well in life needs practice. This is true about work, leisure, science or art. Few people ever find out that they have to practice on themselves in order to mature as a person. This is the central task in the life of every man or woman.

For the student, the most important step is to make the transfer from practicing the method to living—day by day. The only real difference is that there is no longer a teacher with him and the training activities are replaced by activities of everyday life. Otherwise, the process is the same: First the student recognizes a conflict. He pays attention to it and gets in touch with his "holding on"—which represents his defeatist attitude. Then he does what he has already learned to do, he lets go of himself. By practicing this process (from "holding on" to "letting go") the student learns to go with his conflict. He moves toward a more vital attitude. As he achieves harmony with his conflict, the conflict is resolved. He has liberated himself!

A Vitality Exploration—'Shaking is Alright'

After running from physician to physician and trying everything from psychiatry to astrology, Mrs. Miller ended up in my office several weeks ago. ''My biggest problem,'' she said ''is hypoglycemia.'' But as she went on, she talked more and more about her husband and less about herself. She thought he should come and work with me. And on her second visit, she brought him with her. Apparently she had coerced him many times before into going through all the remedies she sought for herself. You didn't have to be an expert to see that Mrs. Miller ran the show. Her free-floating anxiety oozed from every pore. When she talked, it was difficult for anyone else to get a word in edgeways. I could see that her husband had given up trying long ago. I said to her at that time, ''Your husband knows now where he can find me. If he experiences the need to come, he will. But right now I am ready to help you work on yourself.''

It was a long up-hill struggle for Mrs. Miller. She was tempted to stop her work many times, but somehow kept on with it and finally started making real progress. Then she caught on to the energy explorations and through them was able to relax whenever her anxiety rose to a threatening level. With the breathing explorations it was a different story. She seemed to hold onto her breath, too scared to let go of herself. After taking a couple of deep breaths, she would begin to get restless, start scratching herself, twitching her face and most important, break the breathing rhythm altogether! Then she would start talking again, rambling on and on about her hypoglycemia and the troubles she had with her husband.

At the beginning of our last session we started talking about her experience during our previous appointment. At that time she had gone through quite a few breathing cycles, more really than ever before. Just when she had seemed ready to open up, however, she stopped the breathing routine and refused to go on. We had talked a little about the resistance she must be feeling, but she only stammered and made numerous excuses for herself.

At this subsequent session I wanted to bring her back to the previous experience. After chatting for a bit, I said to her, "Last time you were able to stay with the deep breathing more than ever before. It looked for a moment then as if you were beginning to get in touch with something. Can you remember what it was? "I couldn't figure it out at that time," she replied, "maybe because I was too surprised. But now I think I know. I had the distinct feeling that I might start to shake, and I was afraid that once I began shaking I might not be able to stop. It was a strange feeling—a scary one, really. I was worried that I might lose control of myself. And that's when I stopped breathing.''

"This kind of a reaction is very common," I told her. "But control has two sides. You can be just as much in charge of your *letting go* as your *holding on*. You seem to identify your ability to control yourself with holding on and protecting yourself. Letting go, or shaking in this case, you associate with being out of control, of leaving yourself defenseless. If you shake, you think something is wrong with you. You feel weak and think that you should control yourself or pull yourself together. But there is a different way to look at control, a view that we prefer but one which is more difficult to understand. Our attitude is that you should allow yourself to shake. Instead of telling yourself that you shouldn't shake, tell yourself that shaking is all right. After all, shaking is movement and movement is the freeing of energy which has been bound. If you shake, you move. If you move, you are vital.''

In vitality training we make the distinction between *letting go* and *holding on* rather than between *being in control* and *being out of control*. In Mrs. Miller's case, if she allows herself to shake, energy becomes available to her. She is no longer a tight ball, all bound up. Remember the example we used before of being pulled by both of your arms at the same time in opposite directions? If you resist in both directions, you keep yourself from moving. You're at a complete standstill. If you don't move, you can't change your position. This rigid position will only weaken you, and soon you will be in pain and in danger of being ripped apart. The solution to the problem is really very simple. All you have to do is to give up your resistance to one side and go with it instead. You immediately begin to move. Your energy starts to flow and your pain decreases. You gain control of yourself.

The same principle holds true with your shaking. You have an inner conflict about something. You want to express it, but you want to hold onto it at the same time. Your body wants to shake, but it wants to control the shaking at the same time. This kind of a situation can cost you a lot of energy. It is precisely why so many people are tired so much of the time. Mrs. Miller's shaking is the first hopeful sign of movement, movement out of her double-bind.

During our last session I said to her, "Release yourself to the shaking. Tell yourself that shaking is all right, if shaking is what your body wants to do. Then let go of yourself." Mrs. Miller nodded a couple of times and replied, "I have a feeling I know what you are saying. I would like to try the deep breathing again." So I asked her to lie down and begin with the exploration as soon as she was ready. She started without hesitation. After just five or six deep breaths, I could see that she inhaled deeper than ever before. And that she was using her diaphragm more and more in her breathing. She still was a bit restless, and at one point I asked her to relax her face, her neck and her hands with each exhalation. After about thirty deep breaths, I could see her shivering a couple of times and then her body began to quiver. I assured her that she was all right and encouraged her to go through five more cycles. Then I said, "Pay attention to the tingling and the vibrations you feel in your body. Allow yourself to go with them, encourage them and pay attention to them." At that very moment her tears started to flow.

After she had wept for a short while, she turned to me and said, "I know I've been too critical of my husband in the last few years. I guess it was my constant nagging that drove him into the affair he had last year. And yet when I discovered that he was seeing another woman, it almost killed me. I know he stopped seeing her but since then we've become even more distant with each other. I wanted desperately to win him back, but I only seem to drive him further away. I see now what I'm doing. I guess I'd better stop working on him and start learning what's really bothering me."

THE PROJECT

About Groups and Programs

Vitality training is successful only if you are able to transfer your vital attitude into everyday life. By living your vital attitude, you not only enrich your own life, but you serve as a model for other older people around you. Your strength lies in the way you live. If several people like you team up and form a group, the vital power of each member will be even greater. I am referring not only to vitality training groups, but to groups in general which are organized to improve the quality of life for older men and women.

To form your own group, all it takes is a vital attitude, initiative and action. You and one other person who is ready to move forward can start such a group. The two of you then contact some of your older friends and start getting together on a regular basis to share your mutual concerns and aspirations. Our method provides you with a way of supporting one another and will assist each individual in finding a solution to his own particular problem.

After your group has met several times, go out and

find a sponsor. Groups I know have been sponsored by neighborhood associations, adult communities, convalescent hospitals, senior housing units,the YWCA and YMCA, the Red Cross and various other organizations. They all have one thing in common: a vital attitude and a positive approach toward growing old. I know from experience that it is not difficult to find resource people who gladly offer their services to older adults. I have participated in many workshops on massage, nutrition, cooking, dental care, mental health, insomnia, alcoholism that were organized by older adults and supported by local professionals. In the appendix is a list of books which might be useful in providing you with additional ideas and methods for group organization.

I recently read a review in a newspaper about a fiery 90-pound woman, a retired YWCA secretary, who was organizing a group of older people, mostly grey-haired women like herself. She was evidently a powerful orator who kept her audience spell-bound as she related her plans for getting her group off the ground. One reporter said after she had finished talking, "I really can't see how you could miss. I'm sure you will pull off your plans. More power to you! You gals have all the push of panthers!" Her blue eyes darted back at him and she answered excitedly, "I like what you just called us. Our coalition name is too long anyway. From now on, let's be the *Gray Panthers*!"

Today, the Gray Panthers are one of many groups organized to bring about change for the long-living. And their success lies in finding their own solutions rather than waiting for someone else to do it for them. Because they act independently, their own energy is activated. The therapeutic aspect of such an undertaking is in the active participation in which positive attitudes toward life are expressed—not to mention all the practical advantages that arise from the efforts of an organization like this.

During a recent visit to Florida, we came across an example of what older people's political action can accomplish. We had a stop-over at the airport in Tampa. This complex is a perfect example of what the voting power of older adults can do. It is specifically designed for the needs of older people. Distance between points is drastically reduced for departures and arrivals. The building is vertical rather than horizontal as are most airport buildings. The flight gates themselves are laid out in a circular fashion and are connected with the main lobby by moving horizontal "buses." There were a number of empty wheelchairs waiting at each entrance for those who were no longer ambulatory. Furthermore, shuttle cars ran back and forth throughout the complex and had doors large enough to accommodate three wheelchairs at a time. All in all, I would say that people could get around this air terminal with a minimum of walking! And because the risk of older adults hijacking airplanes is minimal, there are no time-consuming security gates. The older adults in Tampa had instigated the design of a specific public facility for the explicit convenience of their own age group. By assuming a positive approach to life, they invested their energies toward making their own world a better place in which to live.

Quite a few programs and organizations for older people are already in operation. A new federal agency was created in 1971 to provide a wide range of meaningful and satisfying activities for older adults—and it was given the appropriate name of ACTION! RSVP, the Retired Senior Volunteer Program, is a part of ACTION. The organization also offers retired people many and varied opportunities to be of service to others in the communities in which they live. Funds to support the program are provided by the federal government and are made available to both public agencies and to private non-profit organizations to fund volunteer programs for persons over age 60. RSVP is not only locally supported, but locally controlled, planned, and operated. Volunteers from RSVP work in libraries, hospitals, nursing homes, correctional institutions and other service agencies. New careers thus open up for older people which can assist them in a very positive way in expressing their own ideas, applying their talents, and challenging their ingenuity and imagination.

Other agencies funded by ACTION which create volunteer opportunities for older adults are: VISTA (Peace Corps Volunteer Service to America), the Foster Grandparent Program, SCORE (the Service Corps of Retired Executives), ACE (the Active Corps of Executives), and the University Year for ACTION.

The Age Discrimination Employment Act (ADEA) is now a Federal law which seeks to prevent employers from discriminating against any persons because of age. This law has helped in many instances to reinstate employees who were retired against their own wishes. It also examines job screening procedures and assists older adults who wish to continue to work.

The Bureau of Outdoor Recreation (BOR) has developed a nationwide outdoor recreation plan for the acquisition and development of resources created specifically for the benefit of older adults. Studies are also under way to improve the services of recreation facilities already available.

Just recently, the Old American Act of 1973 became law. It extends some ongoing programs and adds new initiatives to strengthen government commitments to older adults. Some of the more important provisions of this law are:

1. The Older American Community Service Employment Program, which directly provides parttime jobs for unemployed low-income persons over age 55. Jobs provided are in the field of community service activities such as social, health, welfare, education, library and recreational services. Jobs are also made available in the areas of conservation, maintenance and restoration of natural resources, community betterment and beautification, anti-pollution and environmental quality efforts, and economic development.

2. The Foster Grandparents Program, which includes services to adults as well as to children. Older workers are now able to act as health aides, for example, to persons receiving

home health care or nursing care, and as senior companions for persons having developmental disabilities.

3. The Multi-purpose Senior Center Program, which provides for the acquisition, alteration, and renovation of such centers. The term "Multi-purpose Senior Center Program," as interpreted in the law, means a community facility for the organization and provision of a variety of services for older adults. Grants by the Federal Government to local agencies cover the staffing of these centers.

4. The establishment of Older Reader Service Programs, which make grants available to local agencies to train librarians to work with older adults in the establishment of special library programs; to provide visits by librarians to facilities occupied by older adults; and to hire older adults as library assistants.

5. The State and Community Programs on Aging, which assist local and state agencies to concentrate resources for the development of comprehensive and coordinated service systems to serve older adults.

The opportunities are here. And the message is clear: unite with older people, wherever you are, to take advantage of what has been made available to you. All you need is a vital attitude. Heaven helps those who help themselves!

I don't want to close this section without mentioning the outstanding work which is being done by the National Council on Aging. This association was formerly known as the National Committee on the Aging of the National Social

Welfare Assembly. At that time the Committee made the first nation-wide assessment of the day center movement throughout the country — both as a resource for the elderly and for the communities in which they were established. The National Institute of Senior Centers is now an integral part of the program of the National Council — and serves centers throughout the country on all aspects of organization and legislation. All urban areas have one or more senior centers. The National Council certainly made an outstanding contribution to the development of centers not only here but abroad. The Vitality Training Association is a member of the National Council on Aging.

Vitality Training for Teachers

As a teacher you are not concerned with what your student knows, or what he has, but with who he is. It is not the dis-ease of the student that requests your assistance, but the student himself as a human being. The emphasis then is on the human entity rather than on abnormalities, disease patterns or any treatment techniques. The teacher in vitality training has nothing to do with pathology. That is clearly the job of experts in the helping professions. The teacher, as the word indicates, is an educator, or better yet, in this case, a facilitator. He assists another human being in getting in touch with his attitude and helps him to change it. He relates not to an illness, but to an individual in search of assistance. The sickness or the problems are secondary.

From the moment the teacher and student meet, a new relationship begins to form. It is the most important part of the training process. The relationship is that of one seeking assistance and one who is ready to serve him. The teacher becomes an instrument of the student, and at no time should he consider himself to be a healer. His only role is to get in tune with the student and support the student's vital attitude.

Vitality training reminds me very much of a game we used to play in Austria when I was an instructor at a ski lodge. One person was blindfolded and had to find a needle that had been hidden in the room while he waited outside. He was entirely on his own except that he could hold the hand of another person who knew where the needle was hidden. Although this other person did not *try* to offer any assistance, he somehow provided the searcher with clues about the needle's whereabouts. He unconsciously expressed some resistance through his hand whenever the blindfolded person came near to the needle. By tuning in to this resistance, the searcher was able to eventually locate the hidden needle. It always surprised me how even the most naive person could utilize another's body language to aid them in this way.

In vitality training a similar principle is in operation. The teacher plays the role of the blindfolded person while the student is the one who holds his hand. The hidden needle represents the student's problem of living. The student somehow knows what the problem is but at the same time tries to keep himself and the teacher from discovering it. This is how he creates his conflict. And just as the blindfolded person is able to pick up on this resistance and find the needle, so the teacher tunes into the resistance of the student and helps him to expose his problem.

The student has the solution but he keeps it from himself. For one reason or another he avoids confronting this issue. The teacher, serves the student by supporting him on the basis of the clues, movement, gestures, and words he receives from him. He follows the resistance of the student and asks him to express everything he experiences within himself: his motions, his emotions, his sensations, his images and his hunches. This way the teacher concentrates on supporting the vital attitude of the student, since his defeatist attitude resists all healing. The resistance of the student then, is always directed against the teacher simply because the teacher is identified with the vital attitude. I have never seen an exception. And it is this aspect of the training process which provides the teacher with the clues on which to operate. He can follow and trace the resistance because it is always easier to recognize a resistance that is openly aimed at himself than one which is randomly expressed or concealed.

The greatest danger the teacher faces is in becoming defensive himself during the training process. The student is never disturbed enough not to recognize this and he will use it always to strengthen his defeatist attitude. The best way for a teacher to learn to serve is by getting in touch with his own personal resistance. In order to serve well, he should know as much about himself as possible—his own idiosyncrasies and weaknesses. It is not so important that he resolve all of them —for who can do that?—but that he expose them whenever they are recognized. Trying to hide them from others and, even worse, trying to hide them from himself will destroy his function as a teacher.

Personal growth and fulfillment in the vitality training process is a two-way road. There is much personal satisfaction to be found in the teaching position, in assisting the student to come closer to his own humanity. In the full circle, though, the student himself is also a teacher. And it is through the student that the teacher in the long run grows as a person and replenishes his own vitality.

RECOMMENDED READING

Basic Books

Breathe Away Your Tension, Bruno Geba, Random House/Bookworks, 1973. The first Vitality Training Association handbook introducing exercises in vitality training techniques, including breath awareness, relaxation, energy explorations and massage.

Vigor Regained, Dr. Herbert A. Devries, Prentice-Hall, 1974. Exercise and self-exam techniques for renewed physical vigor for those over 60.

The Well-Body Book, M. Samuels, M.D. & H. Bennett, Random House/ Bookworks, 1973. Simple tools and techniques for self-health care.

Be Well, M. Samuels, M.D. & H. Bennett, Random House/Bookworks, 1974. A system for learning how to stay well.

the first book of *Do-In,* Jacques de Langre, Happiness Press. Pressure point therapy for improved circulation.

Guide to Yoga Meditation, Richard Hittleman, Bantam, 1969.

Guide to Yoga, Richard Hittleman, Bantam, 1969, Elementary guides, simple and easy to follow.

Stories The Feet Have Told, Eunice Ingham Stopfel, P.O. Box 948, Rochester, N.Y. 14603, 1959. Self-healing through foot massage and zone therapy.

One Bowl, Don Gerrard, Random House/Bookworks, 1974. A beginner's guide to food awareness.

Advanced Books

Awareness Through Movement, M. Feldenkrais, Harper & Row, 1972.

Body & Mature Behavior, M. Feldenkrais, International Universities Press, Inc. 1949.

The Alexander Technique, Wilfred Barlow, Knopf, 1974.

Body Time, Gay Luce, Bantam, 1973.

The Stress of Life, H. Selye, McGraw-Hall, 1956.

Sense Relaxation, B. Guenther, MacMillan, 1971.

Better Eyesight Without Glasses, W.H. Bates, Pyramid, 1943.

Living Your Dying, S. Keleman, Random House/Bookworks, 1974.

On Death and Dying, Kubler-Ross, MacMillan, 1970.

Nutrition Almanac, Nutrition Search, John O. Kirschmann, Director,
    706 Second Ave. South, Minneapolis, Minn. 55402, 1973.
Awareness, John Stevens, Bantam, 1973.
New Body, New Mind, Barbara Brown, Harper & Row, 1974.
How To Be Your Own Best Friend, Newman and Berchowitz, Random
    House, 1973.
I'm O.K. Your O.K., Thomas Harris, M.D., Harper & Row, 1967.
Sexual Life After Sixty, Isadore Rubin, Basic Books, 1965.
Food is Your Best Medicine, Henry Bieler, Vintage, 1973.
Patterns of Health, Westlake, Shambhala Publications, 1973.
Senior Power; Growing Old Rebelliously, Paul Kleyman, Glide Publica-
    tions, 1974.
Nobody Ever Died of Old Age, Sharon R. Curtin, Little, Brown, 1973.
The Coming of Age, Simone De Deauvoir, Paperback Library, 1973.

For further information regarding the ideas in this book or the Vitality
Training Association, please write to: Vitality Training Association,
P.O. Box 3365, San Rafael, California 94902.